JESUS LOVES ME, THIS I KNOW

DEVOTIONS FOR FAMILIES
WITH CHILDREN

BY ROLF E. AASENG

DESIGNED AND ILLUSTRATED
BY DON WALLERSTEDT

AUGSBURG PUBLISHING HOUSE
MINNEAPOLIS, MINNESOTA

JESUS LOVES ME, THIS I KNOW

First paperback edition 1977

Copyright © 1973 Augsburg Publishing House

Library of Congress Catalog Card No. 72-90253

International Standard Book No. 0-8066-1572-9

Scripture quotations are from the Revised Standard Version of the Bible, copyright 1946 and 1952 by the Division of Christian Education of the National Council of Churches, and are used by permission.

MANUFACTURED IN THE UNITED STATES OF AMERICA

CONTENTS

A Word to Parents 5

First Choice 6

Come to the Party 9

The Hairs of Your Head 12

Through the Roof 14

Peace 16

Don't Get Rusty 19

A Test Question 21

Strained Gnats 24

Less Than a Penny 26

Dirty Cups 29

Who's Number One? 31

The Son Said 'No' 33

More Than a Mummy 35

Hurrah! 37

Robbers in the Temple 40

Dirty Feet 43

Reminded by a Rooster 46

Sleepy Disciples 49

Who Are You Looking For? 52

A Phony Friend 54

An Enemy's Ear 57

One Answer 59

More Questions 61

Pilate Guessed Wrong 63

Games 66

King on a Cross 69

Forgiven 71

Two Robbers 73

Mother 76
Alone 78
Thirsty 80
Finished 83
Into the Unknown 85
When Bad Is Good 88
A Convinced Soldier 90
Out of the Ground 92
The Best News 95
Empty 98
Unexpected 101
Too Good to Be True 104
Behind Locked Doors 106
Proof 109
A Time to Praise 111
Advance Agent 114
Together 116
A Supper to Remember 118
Forty Days 121
The Best Reminder 124
Wind and Fire 126
A Good Wind 129
Lord 131
3,000 Baptisms 133
People Gifts 136
Something for God 138
Witnesses 140
A Command 142

A WORD TO PARENTS

Every child who has been to Sunday school knows "Jesus Loves Me." This book is intended to give greater substance to that assurance —to provide examples from the Bible of what Jesus has done because of his love for us, and to suggest what meaning this may have in our lives. Many of the devotions deal with the suffering, death, and resurrection of Jesus. You may find them especially valuable for use during the Lent, Easter, and Pentecost seasons, although the book is intended for use at any time of the year.

Some people may be uneasy about discussing the death of Jesus with small children. But it can be helpful to talk about this important part of our faith in the informal setting of family devotions where questions can be dealt with understandingly as they arise.

It is important to read the Bible reference with each devotion. The other elements may be used or adapted in any way you find helpful. The opening sentence of each devotion is intended to provoke discussion prior to the reading of the devotion. Encourage children to read the Scripture or parts of the devotions. Feel free to make up your own questions and prayers as well as things to do. You may wish to include songs and hymns in your devotional period also.

This book is offered with the prayer that through these brief looks at the Bible accounts of the life of Jesus, children and parents alike may find increasing assurance that "Jesus loves me, this I know."

FIRST CHOICE

How do you become someone's friend?

When two people are choosing up sides for a game, somebody in the group has to be the last one picked. If you have ever been the last, or almost the last one to be chosen for a team in this way, you know how unhappy it makes you feel. All you can do is stand and wait, while one after another is chosen before you. You wonder if your name will ever be called; you begin to think that they would rather not have you on their team at all. You like to be wanted. All of us do. We like to have others think highly of what we can do.

When Jesus asks people to be on his team, he doesn't make anyone wait till everyone else is chosen. And you don't have to worry about whether he wants you or not. He makes it very clear that he wants everyone to be on his side.

Even before you know anything about him or his love, or how great

6

it would be to be with him on his team, he has already chosen you. He decided he wanted you with him before you were even born. You are his first choice.

Jesus has chosen you to help carry out his work. It isn't because he feels sorry for you. He expects you to be a valuable member of his team. And he'll appreciate whatever you do.

Jesus has chosen you, whoever you are, to be his friend. He could have commanded you to be his servant, but he'd rather have you as his friend.

Anyone who has ever heard of Jesus surely would like to have him as a friend. He is wise, strong, and kind. But it takes two to be friends. And sometimes the people we would like to have as friends don't want to be our friends. We don't have to worry about that with Jesus. He wants you for his friend even more than you want him—strange as that seems.

What shows this more than any-thing else is that Jesus came to our world to show us God's love. He loved us so much that he even died for us. He came so that we could be his friends.

Jesus wants to be everyone's friend.

Bible reading: John 15:13-16

Why would you like Jesus to be your friend? When did Jesus choose you for his friend? What has Jesus done so we can be his friends?

We thank you, Jesus, that you have chosen us to be your friends. We want to be your friends, too. Help us to be good friends. Amen.

A verse to remember:

"You did not choose me, but I chose you" (John 15:16).

COME TO THE PARTY

Think of a special meal you have attended. What made it special?

Jesus sometimes compared his kingdom to a feast, that is, to a banquet, or a dinner party. Why do you suppose he did this?

Maybe it was because a banquet is something special. When Jesus asks us to attend his party we can be sure he has something good for us. He invites us to be with him forever; he wants to care for us and give us what we need.

Jesus may have talked about a dinner party because it is fun. We enjoy the good food and have fun with people we like and admire. Mealtime is a happy time and we know that being with Jesus will mean happy times with his friends and ours.

Yet some people whom Jesus invites to his party don't want to come. Perhaps they haven't heard or don't understand what Jesus wants to give them. They seem to

think they can get along without him—that what they want is more important than what Jesus wants to give them.

But there will still be a crowd at Jesus' party. You're never alone when you're with Jesus. He wants us all there. Not just the rich or the popular. Everybody. Even those who have never been invited to anything before. Jesus wants us all with him.

Maybe Jesus talked about banquets because a banquet is usually a celebration of some kind. His party is to celebrate the victory he has won over everything that is wrong or bad. He has won this victory for us and he wants us to be a part of the celebration.

We can be at Jesus' banquet now by asking his help in what we do, by letting him rule our lives. He takes care of those who let him. It's great to be a follower of Jesus!

Bible reading: Matthew 22:1-10

Why do you think Jesus talked about his kingdom as a banquet? Why don't some people want to come to it? What do you think is the best part about being in Jesus' kingdom?

Thank you, Jesus, for inviting us to your banquet. Keep us from making excuses to stay away. Show us how to enjoy the good things you have for us. Amen.

Something to do:

Plan a celebration in your family that you think Jesus would like to attend. Decide what to celebrate (a birthday, a new job, a new baby, good grades, new friends, an anniversary), whom to invite, and what you can do to make it a happy time for everybody—including mother.

11

THE HAIRS
OF
YOUR HEAD

How many hairs do you have on your head?

There probably isn't anyone who knows how many hairs he has on his head—unless he is very bald. It might be possible to count our hairs if we wanted to take the time. But it wouldn't do much good. By the time we finished, our count would probably be wrong. For we're losing hair all the time, and we don't even notice it. A few hairs are of no value. The hairs on our head aren't worth counting.

Yet Jesus says God knows how many hairs we have. He doesn't mean that God keeps a record book filled with entries like these: "John grew two new hairs, so now he has 86,758." "Mary lost five so she has 89,004." "Rusty has 78,406." What Jesus means is that God is concerned about us, even about things that we don't think are worth much. Even though he is the powerful ruler of the whole universe, with all the stars and planets under his control, he is still concerned about the little things, like losing a few hairs, that could disturb our lives.

Jesus talked about everyday sparrows, too. They aren't worth much either. You can buy two of them for a penny, Jesus said. We would have a hard time finding anyone who would want to buy sparrows even at that price. Yet, says Jesus, God takes notice when one of these most common birds dies.

Jesus tells us that we don't need to worry about what might happen to us. We are worth much more than a sparrow. We are worth more than a whole bushel of hairs. If God cares about things of such little value, surely he cares even more about what happens to the people he has created. He'll take care of us. He loves us.

We are worth something to God. He loves us and the whole world so much that he sent Jesus to live and to die for us. We can be sure God will take care of us.

Bible reading: Matthew 10:29-31

How much is a sparrow worth? Why do you think Jesus said God knows how many hairs we have on our head? How much are you worth to God?

We thank you, God, for sending Jesus to bring us your love. Help us to be sure of your love for us every day. Amen.

Something to do:

Think of something that has very little value, but which God takes care of (it might be a plant or animal). Think of ways you can help to care for it.

13

THROUGH THE ROOF

How much would you do to help a friend be healed of an illness?

Four men had a sick friend. They were sure Jesus could heal him. But so many people had crowded into the house where Jesus was that they couldn't even get inside the door. So they came through the roof.

It wasn't quite as bad as it sounds. The houses were low and had flat roofs. They were built of stone and mud or tiles. So it wasn't too hard to climb up on the roof and remove some tiles.

The men made a hole in the roof large enough to let their friend through on a stretcher. Carefully they lowered him by ropes until he was right in front of Jesus. Then they waited for Jesus to heal him. Instead Jesus looked at the man and said, "Your sins are forgiven."

These words made some of the people in the crowded room angry. "What's the idea of saying that?"

14

they grumbled. "Only God can forgive sins."

But Jesus answered, "Which is easier, to say 'Your sins are forgiven,' or to say, 'Get up and walk?' "

Then Jesus told the man, "Get up from your stretcher and go back to your house." And the man stood right up, completely healed. By doing this miracle, Jesus hoped the people would come to believe that he could not only cure sickness, but that he could also forgive sins.

We are willing to go to a great deal of trouble and expense to bring sick friends and relatives to good doctors so they can get well. How often do we think of bringing friends to Jesus so they can be cured of sin?

By forgiving this man's sins first, Jesus showed us that he thinks sin is our greatest problem. But he has taken our sins away by his death on the cross. And he has the power to heal our sickness too.

Bible reading: Mark 2:1-12

What did the people have to do to get to Jesus? Why? What did Jesus tell the man first? Why do you think he did this? Which is more important, to be healed of disease, or to have our sins forgiven?

Thank you, Jesus, for forgiving our sins and for giving us health. Amen.

A verse to remember:

"If we confess our sins, he is faithful and just, and will forgive our sins" (1 John 1:9).

If someone asked you to draw a picture showing what peace means, what would you draw?

PEACE

Once an artist was asked to paint a picture of peace. People no doubt expected him to paint a quiet pond in the woods, or a garden with flowers and bushes and a fountain, or fluffy clouds floating above a meadow on a summer day.

He surprised them, for his painting showed a furious storm. It looked anything but peaceful. But in the middle of the wind and water, safe behind a rock, perched a little bird. The bird knew it was safe, even in a storm, because it was protected by the rock. It was at peace.

One of the good things Jesus gives us is peace. It may not always be what we expect. Peace doesn't mean that things will always go along smoothly for us, or that we'll have no trouble. Many things in the world can cause us problems; we can't possibly avoid them all.

On the other hand, even if people seem quiet on the outside, we cannot be sure that they have peace. Someone may be upset about something even though others may not know anything is wrong. And if you don't feel good on the inside, you aren't at peace.

Jesus said that the kind of peace he gives us isn't like the peace the world gives. It's different because it comes from God, not men.

Often he can help people to settle their differences peacefully. But his peace doesn't depend on how well we can stay away from trouble. Jesus can give us peace in spite of our mistakes and the wrong that others might do to us.

The peace Jesus gives gets down inside us. It takes away our worries, our anger, our dislikes. We can have peace even when troubles are all around us.

The reason Jesus can give such peace is that he has won out over everything that can make life stormy. He has defeated sin and

evil by rising from the dead, and to us he says, "My peace I give to you."

When we know that, we are at peace, no matter how many troubles and storms come to our lives. We are protected by Jesus.

Bible reading:

John 14:27; 16:32-33

What has Jesus done to give us peace? What is different about the peace he gives? What can we do to help others have this peace?

Thank you, Jesus, for winning the battle over sin and giving us peace. Help us to share your peace with others. Amen.

Something to do:

Think of a way you could spread peace to someone else, at home or in school or in church.

DON'T GET RUSTY

Among the people you know, who can do the most things well? Who do you think is the most helpful to others? Are they the same person?

Some children are good ball players; others can play a musical instrument. Some can do both. Others may not be good at sports or music, but they can cook or work out the answers to hard problems.

Some can't do any of these things. They may feel they aren't good at anything. But if you look into it, you'll probably find that they can do something no one has thought about. Maybe they can train a dog to do tricks, or take care of a baby brother, or keep a room looking neat.

The ability to do something well we call a talent. Some people have many talents; they can do many things well. Others are good at only a few things, or maybe only one. But God has given everyone some talent. No one can say there is nothing he can do.

When we use our talents, our ability improves. If we can sing, the more we sing the better we sound. If we can play ball, the more we practice the better we can play.

Many people try to use the talents God has given them, whether many or few, to help other people. Others don't want to do anything for someone else. But when they don't use their talent they begin to lose it. Sometimes we say they get rusty, just like a piece of machinery. If you leave a machine unused, it gets rusty and soon doesn't work.

It takes time to discover what we can do best and how we can use our talents. School helps us to learn what we can do and what we like to do. We can be sure that there is something we can do for God with the abilities he has given us. We can use our talents now to help others. The more we use them, the happier we are and the better we can serve God.

Bible reading: Matthew 25:14-29

What happens when you use your talents? What happens when you don't use them? What is one talent God has given you? Have you thought about a way to use your life for God?

Thank you, Jesus for the abilities you have given us. Help us to know what we can do best and then to use our talents to help others. Amen.

Something to do:

Pick out one talent each member of your family has. Talk about how you can improve it, and how you can use this talent to help others.

Which is the most important of the Ten Commandments?

A TEST QUESTION

People were always giving Jesus tests. They didn't do it in a school classroom, but as Jesus traveled from place to place, people often asked him questions. They were testing him to see what kind of a teacher he was, to see if he was worth listening to. Some who asked questions were hoping they could trick him into saying something wrong so they could tell people not to listen to him.

One of the test questions they asked him was, "Which of the Ten Commandments is the most important?" The person who asked the question may have thought that no matter what commandment Jesus picked, it would be easy to find somebody who would think he should have chosen a different one. Then the questioner would try to turn that person against Jesus.

But Jesus had an answer that he wasn't expecting. The greatest

commandment, said Jesus, is to love God above everything. Then he added, "There is a second commandment that is just as important: Love your neighbor. All the other commandments depend on these two."

The man who asked the question couldn't find anything wrong with Jesus' answer.

Love for God and love for other people go together. If we really love God, we want to love everybody we meet, because God loves everyone. If we want to do something for other people, we want to have God's help, for he can do the most for us and them.

We have to answer the same question Jesus did, although it may be asked in a different way. What do we think is really important in our life? The answer Jesus gave is still the best one.

Most of the time we answer that question by what we do. We show whether we love God by the way we act. If we love God we'll do what he wants. And that means helping our neighbors.

Bible reading: Matthew 22:34-40

Why did people ask Jesus questions? What did he say was the most important commandment? How do we show what we think is most important in our life?

To love you, Father, is the most important thing in our lives. Help us to grow in our love for you, and to show that love by loving people as you do. Amen.

A verse to remember:

"You shall love the Lord your God with all your heart, and with all your soul, and with all your mind" (Matt. 22:37).

STRAINED GNATS

Have you ever swallowed a gnat?

Gnats are little bugs that often swarm around your face in the summer time, especially out in the woods, and sometimes even in your back yard. They're so small that you might not notice them, except that they often gather in large numbers just over your head, and they seem to insist on flying into your face.

If you've swallowed one, it's not because you wanted to, but because you couldn't help it. Gnats are so small, and there are so many of them, and they come buzzing up so close, that it isn't at all strange if one of them ends up inside you.

But I'm sure you have never swallowed a camel!

Yet this is the example Jesus once used. "You strain out a gnat and swallow a camel," he said. The meaning is, "You make sure you pick out all the tiny little bugs,

24

yet a huge beast like a camel you don't even notice!"

He was talking about people who make a big fuss over things that aren't very important, but pay no attention to what is really important. They may be upset if their pastor grows a beard, but never listen to what he says. They may complain about the hymns they sing in church, but rarely do anything that would make another person feel like singing. They may be very fussy about keeping weeds out of their lawn, but they let bad habits like telling lies or being rude grow in their lives. They may criticize a person who doesn't belong to church, but when he joins they never speak to him. They may handle the Bible very carefully, but do not read it and pay no attention to what it teaches. They may be sure to send valentines to every person in the class, but are friendly only to a few and make fun of others.

That's straining gnats and swallowing camels. It's easy to do.

Jesus always gave first place to his Father and to the needs of people. He offers us his love so we can do the same.

Bible reading: Matthew 23:23-24

What did Jesus mean when he said people strain out a gnat and swallow a camel? Can you think of any "camels" you've swallowed? How can we decide which are the important things in life and which are less important?

Dear Jesus, help us to know what is important and to put first things first. Amen.

Something to do:

Make a list of the "camels," the important things, you have been forgetting in your life, and of the "gnats," the little things you've paid too much attention to. Plan how you can give more attention to the important things.

LESS THAN A PENNY

What is the best gift you ever received? What do you suppose is the largest gift ever given to your church?

Often the gifts we like the best are those that cost the most money. Jesus measures things differently.

Once he and his disciples were watching people put money into a box at the temple. They didn't pass offering plates during the service in those days, as we do. Instead, whenever anyone wanted to give something to God's work, he would put it into a special box. Sometimes people stood close by to watch how much money each one gave.

One day several people came by to put something in the box. Some were rich and put in large amounts of money. Then along came a poor widow. She put in a very small amount, two coins worth less than a penny. But when Jesus saw it he said to his disciples, "This poor woman gave a larger gift than any of those rich men."

26

His words must have sounded strange to the disciples. Jesus explained what he meant by saying that the others put in what they could afford. Even if they gave a large amount they had plenty of money left over.

This poor woman, on the other hand, put in all she had. She loved God so much and wanted so badly to give a gift to him that she put in her last bit of money. She didn't even stop to wonder where she would get more to buy food. She trusted God to take care of her.

Jesus spoke of her as an example of faith and love. At another time Jesus said that if we put God first, he will bless us with everything we need to live. God is pleased when we give to his church because we want to, whether the amount is small or large. He treasures most the gifts people give him because they love him.

Bible reading: Mark 12:41-44

Who did Jesus say had put in the most money? How much had she put in? Why did Jesus think that was so much? How should we decide how much to give to the church or other causes?

We know that you have given us everything we have, Lord. We want to give something to you too. Help us to share with love. Amen.

Something to do:

Decide on some special gift you can give that you think will please Jesus.

Do you think it is easy to make people think you are better than you really are?

DIRTY CUPS

Suppose your mother gave you some cups to wash. But you got lazy and decided to wash only the outside of those cups. Then you put them in the cupboard as if they were ready to use again.

You wouldn't get away with that for long! As soon as your mother found them you would be washing those dirty cups again. And it wouldn't do any good to say, "But they look clean enough on the shelf."

Your mother would say, "That isn't enough. Look at the inside. That's what counts." No matter how nice it might look on the shelf, no one wants to use a cup that is dirty on the inside.

Jesus said some people are like a cup that has been washed only on the outside. He was talking about people who like to pretend they are better than they are. They may join a church and act like other church members when they are around them. But they don't really believe what the church teaches. And when they are away from church they don't act like Christians at all.

A person seeing them only in church on Sunday might think they are good Christians. They look all right from the outside. But inside it is a different thing. They don't really care about God. It doesn't bother them to do wrong. They aren't interested in helping others.

They may fool people, but not God. He knows what they are like on the inside. To join a church or some other good organization doesn't change people on the inside. Nothing we do can take away our sin, and sin spoils our whole life. Only God can do anything about that. The only way we can be clean, inside and out, is for God to take away our sin.

This is exactly what he wants us to do. And when God forgives our sins, we not only look better to people on the outside, but we really are different people inside too.

When God says, "I forgive you," we are forgiven. And we feel clean inside, too.

Bible reading: Matthew 23:25-26

Who did Jesus say are like dirty cups? What does it mean for a person to be clean on the outside? How can we become "clean"?

Forgive us, Father, when we pretend to be better than we are. Make us clean inside and out. Amen.

A verse to remember:

"Though your sins are like scarlet, they shall be as white as snow" (Isaiah 1:18).

Who is the greatest person you can think of? Why do you think he or she is great?

WHO'S NUMBER ONE?

We're Number One!

That's the chant you hear after almost every championship football or basketball game. Cheering fans like to tell everybody that their team is the best in the whole country, or in whatever league they play.

Not only athletic teams like to be Number One. We all like to have people notice us and see how good we are. We like to have people think we're better than others in some way.

Sometimes there may be an argument over who really is Number One. More than one team may claim to be the best. Or more than one person may want the top position. They may list the things they've done, trying to persuade others that they deserve to be called Number One.

Jesus had a strange way of deciding who is Number One. Some would say he had it all backward. For he said the one who serves others the most is the greatest.

Jesus showed what he meant by his life. More than anyone else he could have claimed to be Number One. After all, he was God's Son. There had never been anyone like him. He could do things no one else could do. He could have had any job, any honor, any power he wanted.

But instead of claiming to be Number One, he lived as a poor man in a small town. He never had much money; he didn't have fine clothes or a big house. He had no important job. He didn't travel far or meet great people. His whole life was given to serving other people: helping them, healing them, teaching them—and finally dying for them.

When you stop to think of what Jesus did, there really isn't any argument about who is the greatest person who ever lived. Jesus is Number One because he has done the most for all people.

Bible reading: Matthew 20:25-28

Who did Jesus say was first in his kingdom? What has Jesus done to be Number One? What can we do to be like him?

Help us, Jesus, to follow your example, and to measure our success by how much we can help others. Amen.

Something to do:

Find a newspaper or magazine article about a person who is Number One according to the way Jesus rates people.

Have you ever agreed to do something and then didn't do it? How did you feel about it afterward?

THE SON SAID 'NO'

A father once asked his two sons to mow the lawn. The first one said, "I don't want to." But the other boy said, "Okay, Dad, I'll do it right away."

Which of the two answered in a way that pleased his father? That's easy. The one who agreed to do what his father asked, of course.

But suppose the son who said "okay" never got around to mowing the lawn. He got busy with one thing after another and soon forgot all about his promise. But his brother, who said he didn't want to mow the lawn, began to feel sorry that he had answered his father that way. So without saying anything more, he went to the garage, got out the mower, and cut the lawn.

Jesus told a story something like that, then asked the people who were listening, "Which of the two boys did what his father wanted?" It was an easy question. The people agreed that it was the son who actually did what his father asked, no matter what he had said.

Some people say they are good Christians. They make sure that their names are on the membership list of a church. But they never seem to get around to doing the things Jesus wants his followers to do.

Others make no claims for themselves. They don't feel they are better than anyone else and may even say they don't amount to much. Yet they quietly keep on helping others, being kind, and doing what God wants us to do.

It's not hard to see which people are really doing what God wants. It isn't always what you say that counts.

Bible reading: Matthew 21:28-32

Can you think of some things you have agreed to do, but never got around to doing? What are some of the things Jesus would like us to do for him? How can we keep from forgetting to do them?

God, we're sorry that we sometimes forget to do things we should —and that sometimes we don't even want to do them. Help us to know what you want us to do, and give us a willingness to do it. Amen.

Something to do:

Decide on just one thing you will do for Jesus during the next day—then do it.

**How would you feel if some-
one who had died came to
life again?**

MORE
THAN A
MUMMY

Most people don't like to think
about death or dead people. After
someone has died and been buried,
it gives us a squeamish feeling
even to think about digging up the
body.

Yet this is just what Jesus asked.
His friend Lazarus had died and
had been buried, apparently in a
grave cut into the side of a hill.
Four days later Jesus came to the
place. He told the people to take
away the stone that covered the
opening of the grave.

They were uneasy about doing
this. But Jesus said they should
trust him and they would see something wonderful.

Then Jesus prayed to his Father.
We might think it a strange prayer.
He didn't ask God to do anything.
He just thanked him for always
listening to his prayers. He said he
was praying in this way so the peo-

ple could understand more clearly that he had come from God.

Finally Jesus called out to the man who had been buried, "Lazarus, come out!" Imagine how the people felt when they saw something move in the cave. A figure got up and walked to the entrance. It was Lazarus, all wrapped up like a mummy, the way he had been buried. Jesus told the people to take off the wrappings, and Lazarus was alive and well.

By this great miracle Jesus showed that he has power over death. The people were amazed. Many believed in Jesus because of what he had done. Some made a special trip to this village just to see Lazarus.

Jesus promises that after we die he will bring to life again each one of us who believes in him. And we won't have to die again, as Lazarus did; we can live with Jesus forever.

Bible reading: John 11:38-44

What did Jesus ask the people to do? Why didn't they want to? What can we learn from this miracle?

We're glad, Jesus, that you are powerful enough to bring dead people back to life. We are glad that we can look forward to living with you after we die. Amen.

A verse to remember:

"I am the resurrection and the life" (John 11:25).

When did you last see a pa-rade? What was in it?

HURRAH!

It was a strange parade. No one had held a meeting beforehand to plan it. No one had decided what streets they should march down, or asked the police to block off traffic. There were no marching bands, no soldiers. Not even any floats. Just one man, riding on a little donkey—and crowds of people walking behind, alongside, and in front of him.

The man was Jesus. He and his disciples were going to Jerusalem from the place where they had spent the night. Jesus had sent two disciples to get a donkey for him to ride on. They brought back one that no one had ever ridden before. Since they had no saddle, the disciples put their coats on the donkey. Then Jesus got on and started down the road.

When people saw Jesus riding the donkey, they began to follow him. Others came out of the city to

meet him. Some began to shout and sing, "Hurrah for Jesus! Jesus is our king! He is coming in God's name." Soon most of the people were shouting.

Some of the people broke off branches from nearby palm trees and laid them on the road so Jesus would have a carpet of palm branches to ride on. (That's why we call the day Palm Sunday.) Others even took off their jackets and spread them out on the road in front of Jesus.

A few people thought it was wrong for Jesus to let the people honor him in this way. They told him he shouldn't allow it. But Jesus said it was right for the people to welcome him. For he really is a king. He is the ruler of all the people who have ever lived.

That means he is our king too. And we want to welcome him to our hearts, just as the people welcomed him into Jerusalem.

Bible reading: Matthew 21:1-11

Why do we call the day when Jesus came to Jerusalem Palm Sunday? Why did people shout and wave branches? How can we show that Jesus is our king?

Come into my heart, come into my heart, come into my heart, Lord Jesus. Come in today, come in to stay; come into my heart, Lord Jesus. Amen.

Something to do:

Find a hymn that calls Jesus a king and sing it together.

ROBBERS IN THE TEMPLE

What would you think if you came to church one Sunday and found someone going up and down the aisles selling popcorn, as they do at ball games? Why would you feel that way?

The day after Jesus entered Jerusalem on the donkey, he came back again to visit the temple. What he heard as he came near the temple must have sounded something like a carnival or a ball game—not at all like a church.

In those days people had to give a special coin and certain types of animals as offerings at the temple. Many came from towns far away—even from other countries. These people couldn't bring the special offerings all that distance. So there were little shops right in the temple courtyard where they could buy animals or exchange coins.

Sometimes the owners of these shops made the people pay much more than was right. They were cheating people, and doing it

40

while pretending to help them worship God.

When Jesus saw the people pretending to serve God when really they were trying to get rich by cheating, he became very angry. He told those who were selling things to get out of the temple. Some didn't pay any attention to him, so he began tipping over their tables and boxes to show he really meant business.

When they complained about what he was doing, Jesus told them, "God says, 'My house shall be a house of prayer,' but you have made it a den of robbers." Jesus wants us to remember that our church is God's house. What we do there should always honor God.

Bible reading: Mark 11:15-19

What was going on at the temple? What did Jesus do? Why? What does he want us to remember?

Help us, Father, to use our church, and our lives, for you. Amen.

Something to do:

Collect pictures of different kinds of churches. You might want to make a collection by taking pictures of churches with your own camera.

How do you get ready for a meal before you sit down to eat?

DIRTY FEET

When Jesus lived in Palestine, people washed not only their hands before a meal, but sometimes their feet too. Whenever someone came into his house, the first thing the host, or servant, did was to wash his feet. This was necessary because in those days people wore sandals without stockings and they walked on dirt roads. So their feet would be quite dirty from walking even a short distance.

One night Jesus and his disciples had arranged to eat supper together. They were using someone else's house, and the owner was not present. So he couldn't wash their feet; nor were there any servants. As a result, nobody's feet were washed.

None of the disciples offered to do this job. Perhaps they were thinking, "It isn't my job to wash anybody's feet; I'm not a servant." And of course if everyone felt he

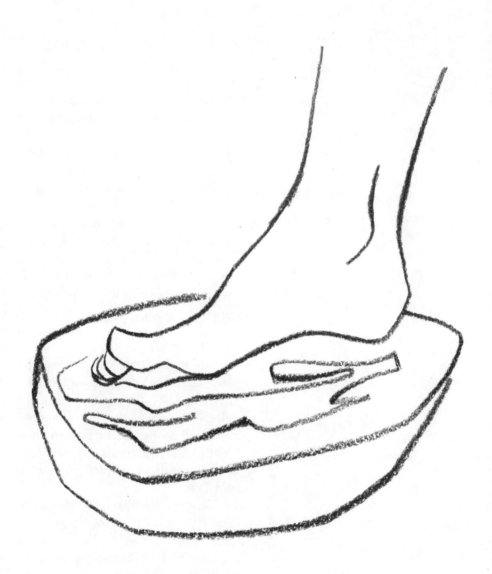

was too good to do this kind of work, it wouldn't get done.

Sometimes we too may think or say, "It's not my job—it's his turn—I don't have to wait on her." And so something good or necessary doesn't get done.

But the disciples' feet were washed that night anyway. Can you guess who did it? It was Jesus. The disciples were ashamed when Jesus brought a pan of water and a towel and began to wash their feet. They knew they should be waiting on him; yet he was washing their feet as though he were their servant.

He told them, just as he tells us, "I want you to do as I have done. Don't expect others to serve you, but see how much you can do for them."

Jesus spent his whole life serving people. He still is doing things for us. He helps us to help others too.

Bible reading: John 13:3-16

What did Jesus do for the disciples? Why was this strange? How can we follow his example?

Forgive us, Lord, for sometimes thinking that we are too good to serve others. Help us to remember how you serve us, and lead us to do helpful things for others. Amen.

A verse to remember:

"Whoever would be great among you must be your servant" (Matt. 20:26).

REMINDED BY A ROOSTER

Has anyone ever tried to keep you from doing something wrong or foolish by warning you? How did you feel about it?

Jesus knew he was going to be taken prisoner by his enemies. He also knew this would scare away even his closest friends. He tried to warn them about what would happen. "You'll all run away tonight when you see what happens to me," Jesus told them. "But I want you to come back to me."

They couldn't understand how this could happen. They wouldn't think of leaving him, their best friend, especially if he were in trouble—although of course they didn't imagine that anyone as wonderful as Jesus could get into trouble.

Each disciple claimed that he was the most loyal. Peter said, "Even if I have to die with you, I won't leave you." He meant it; all of them meant it. But they didn't know the trouble that lay ahead.

46

And maybe they were a little too sure of themselves.

So Jesus warned Peter, "Before you hear the rooster crow twice tonight, you will say three times you don't even know me." But Peter was sure Jesus was wrong.

That night Jesus was taken prisoner. The disciples ran away, just as he had said. But Peter sneaked back to see what would happen to Jesus. A girl saw him and said, "Weren't you with this guy they arrested?"

Peter was frightened and said, "No, I don't even know him." Later two other people asked if he were a friend of Jesus. Both times he said "no."

Then a rooster crowed. Peter remembered what Jesus had said just a few hours earlier. He was so ashamed and sad that he ran out into the street, crying.

He remembered how kind and forgiving Jesus had always been. He hoped that even now Jesus would love him. And Jesus did.

Bible reading: Matthew 26:31-35

Why were the disciples so sure they wouldn't leave Jesus? Can you think of times when you've failed Jesus? What should you do about it when that happens? Does Jesus still love you after you've done something wrong?

Jesus, sometimes we act as though we don't know you. Make us more willing to stand up for what we know is right even when it looks dangerous. And when we fail, help us to come back to you for forgiveness. Amen.

Something to do:

Some people use the figure of a rooster to remind them to remain true to Jesus. Make something for your wall or desk or mantle, using a rooster or some other symbol to remind you of Christ's love for you.

Do you think you'd want to know about it ahead of time if something bad were going to happen to you?

SLEEPY DISCIPLES

Jesus expected that he would be arrested. He tried to warn the disciples about what would happen to him, but they couldn't imagine that he was in any danger.

After they had their last supper together, Jesus asked some of the disciples to stay with him to wait for whatever might happen. They probably didn't expect anything to happen—at least not so soon. Or maybe it was just that it was so late at night. At any rate, when Jesus went off by himself to pray, they soon fell asleep instead of waiting up with him.

This waiting was hard on Jesus too. He knew Judas was busy stirring up trouble for him. More than likely something would happen that very night. Who would come to take him captive, and how would they do it? Would they give him a

trial? He knew his enemies would not treat him gently. And sooner or later they would put him to death in a painful way. It was all so unfair, for Jesus had done nothing wrong. He shouldn't be treated as a criminal. It was not pleasant to think about what might be coming.

So Jesus asked his Father if there were any other way he could carry out his task without going through such suffering. But he knew his Father loved him and would do only what was best. So he added to his prayer, "Don't do what I want, but what you know is best." Leaving it in God's hands helped him to face whatever the future would bring.

Yet Jesus was disappointed when he found his disciples sleeping. He was concerned about what might happen to them. "Watch and pray that you aren't tempted to do wrong," he told them.

That is good advice for us too. And the way Jesus prayed can help us also. When we face a trial, we may ask God to help us out of it. And as Jesus did, we can also say to God, "You do what is right" —and then leave it up to him. For we know God loves us.

Bible reading: Matthew 26:36-46

What made it especially hard for Jesus to face what would happen to him? What did Jesus pray? How can we learn to pray that God will do what is best?

Father, we are thankful that you love us so much that we can safely turn any problem over to you and trust you to do what is best for us. Help us to watch and pray so we won't be tempted to do wrong. Amen.

A verse to remember:

"Not my will, but thine, be done" (Luke 22:42).

51

WHO ARE YOU LOOKING FOR?

Are there times when we should not try to get out of something unpleasant even if we could?

If we had been in Jesus' place the night when he was arrested, we might have acted quite differently from the way he did. We might have tried to run away. There's a good chance that Jesus could have escaped if he had tried. He would have had a good head start because he must have seen the men coming after him when they were quite a distance away; they came into the garden carrying lanterns and swords and must have made a good deal of noise. In addition, it was dark and there were probably trees and bushes to hide behind.

But instead of running or hiding, Jesus walked forward to meet the men who came for him. "Who are you looking for?" he asked them.

"Jesus of Nazareth," they answered.

"I am he," Jesus said.

Rather than coming up and grabbing him, the men shrank back and fell to the ground when he said that. For a fleeting instance, they must have caught a glimpse of God's power in Jesus, and they were afraid. At that moment Jesus could have walked right through the midst of them without harm, as he had done before when people wanted to kill him.

Instead, Jesus asked them again, "Who are you looking for?"

Again they answered, "Jesus of Nazareth."

Jesus said, "I told you before: I'm the one you want. So let the rest of these men go."

Even when he was facing great danger, Jesus was thinking of the safety of his friends. He made sure that his disciples would be safe before he allowed the men to take him prisoner.

For he did allow it; they couldn't have taken him otherwise.

Jesus didn't run; he did not call on angels for help; he did no miracle, because he wanted to help the people of the world. And he knew there was no other way. He let himself be arrested because he loved us.

Bible reading: John 18:3-9

What did the guards do when Jesus said he was the only one they were looking for? Why didn't Jesus run away or try to get out of being arrested?

We thank you, Jesus, for always thinking about the safety of your friends. Amen.

Something to do:

Think of people you are especially concerned about. Make a point to pray for them every day.

Can you think of anyone who pretended to be a friend when he really was an enemy?

A PHONY FRIEND

You don't usually make a friendly call carrying clubs and swords. Yet Judas seemed to be pretending that he was coming as a friend, in spite of the fact that he was with a band of people who were armed as though they were hunting for an escaped murderer. A crowd like that, barging through a park after midnight, isn't likely to be making a neighborly call.

Judas went up to Jesus, called him Master, and kissed him in the usual way for friends to greet each other. He did it so the men with him would be sure to grab the right person in case they didn't know what Jesus looked like, or if there should be confusion. Maybe he hoped his act would fool Jesus— or at least the disciples—so they wouldn't try to fight or run away.

Jesus wasn't fooled, of course. He knew Judas meant nothing by

kissing him or calling him Master. Yet he called Judas a friend, and he meant it. "Friend," he said, "why are you here?"

Jesus knew why Judas was there. Perhaps he was trying to bring Judas to his senses, to help him realize what he was doing by double-crossing a true friend.

Even at this moment, Jesus loved Judas. If Judas had changed his mind, Jesus would have forgiven him and taken him back as a disciple.

Jesus loves us all, even when we do things against him. He does everything he can to help us see that we have been wrong, and to bring us back to him as friends.

Bible reading: Matthew 26:47-50

Why did Judas kiss Jesus? What did Jesus say to him? What could make Jesus stop loving us?

We thank you, Jesus, that no matter what we do, you never stop loving us or trying to help us. If we ever turn against you, help us to remember your love and come back to you. Amen.

Something to do:

Pick out someone in your family or among your friends as your secret friend. Don't tell anyone who it is. Then try to do something kind or helpful for that person as often as you can.

56

Try to think of someone who wanted to defend another person but ended up causing him harm.

AN ENEMY'S EAR

The guards who came to take Jesus prisoner may have expected that they would have a battle on their hands. They knew eleven very loyal men would be with Jesus, men who had said they would die rather than leave him. So the guards came prepared for anything, carrying swords and clubs.

For a while it looked as though they would have their fight. For when they came forward to take Jesus and it became clear that Judas was not there as a friend, Peter took out his sword and swung at the nearest man. He must have ducked, but the sword still cut off his ear.

Ordinarily that would have started a bitter fight; but it was all over as quickly as it began. For Jesus told Peter, "Put your sword away." Not only that, but he reached over and touched the man's ear, and it was healed. How do you suppose that man felt about seizing Jesus then?

When the disciples saw this, they didn't know what to do. They were ready to fight for Jesus, but he wouldn't let them. For Jesus knew that if he was going to help people as he had come to the world to do, he would have to be arrested. And he knew also that you don't win the kind of battles he was fighting by killing or wounding people. So the disciples ran away, as he knew they would, leaving Jesus alone.

There are still people who want to rush in swinging swords—doing things that will hurt people, in order to defend Jesus and his church. They want to defeat the enemies of Jesus and teach them a lesson by punishing them or passing laws against them or doing something to hurt them.

Jesus goes about it in quite a different way. He doesn't want to destroy his enemies. He wants to heal them and turn them into his disciples if possible. For he loves even those who fight against him. That's why he was willing to go without a fight with the men who came to arrest him.

Bible reading: Luke 22:49-54

Who tried to defend Jesus? What did he do? Why didn't Jesus want the disciples to fight? If we want to fight for Jesus what is the best way we can do it?

Help us to understand what you want us to do, Jesus, so we won't come in swinging swords or hurting people when you have a better plan. Amen.

A verse to remember:

"Love your enemies" (Matt. 5:44).

ONE ANSWER

Think of some of the names Jesus used for himself.

When he was brought before the high priest after he had been taken prisoner, Jesus answered only one question. The religious leaders were holding a kind of trial to decide whether Jesus was guilty of a crime. According to the laws, Jesus didn't have to answer the questions they were asking him. It wouldn't have done any good anyway, for these leaders had decided long ago that they were going to put Jesus to death as a criminal.

Why did Jesus answer even one question then? Maybe because he wanted to give even these enemies one last chance to know who he was and to believe in him. For he loved these religious leaders just as much as anyone. He came to die for their sins too. Maybe someone in the courtroom would understand him and believe.

The question he answered was,

"Are you the Christ?" (That meant, Are you the one God through the Old Testament promised to send to be the savior of his people?) "Are you the Son of God?"

Jesus answered, "I am." And he added, "And you shall see with your own eyes that this is true when the Son of Man rules with God in heaven."

The high priest understood at once the tremendous claim Jesus made by this answer. He immediately forgot about trying to prove Jesus had done anything wrong. Instead he declared that the trial was over. Jesus should be killed, these leaders decided, because he claimed to be God.

Perhaps Jesus answered that question for our sake too. It is one of the clearest statements in the Bible in which Jesus tells us in his own words who he is. He is the Son of God. And we too can look forward to seeing the proof of that with our own eyes.

Bible reading: Mark 14:55-64

What question did Jesus answer? Why do you think he answered only that one? Who did Jesus say he was?

Jesus, we are looking forward to seeing you in your heavenly glory. Amen.

Something to do:

Go through the four Gospels to find an answer to the question: Who did Jesus say he was?

MORE QUESTIONS

If Jesus lived among us today, do you think he would be accused of any crimes?

It was a strange way to act in a courtroom.

Jesus was on trial before Pilate, the military ruler and judge in Jerusalem. The high priest and his followers had brought him there after they had declared Jesus guilty. They wanted him killed, and Pilate was the only one who could condemn a person to death.

If Pilate ruled that Jesus was guilty, it would mean his death. Yet Jesus seemed to make no attempt to defend himself or convince Pilate that he was innocent. He didn't seem to be interested in the charges the priests made against him, nor did he answer the questions Pilate asked.

Except once. Pilate had asked, "Are you the king of the Jews?"

Jesus answered, "Does it really make any difference to you?"

When Pilate showed that he

wanted to know something about him, Jesus explained that he did have a kingdom. But it was not the kind of kingdom Pilate served; Christ's kingdom was a kingdom of truth. Jesus seemed to be giving Pilate a chance to be a part of this kingdom.

When Jesus answered no more questions, Pilate became irritated and said, "Don't you know I have power to let you live or to put you to death?"

Jesus answered simply, "You wouldn't have any power at all unless someone allowed you to have it." He was talking about God, who was allowing Pilate to make up his own mind about Jesus. God doesn't force people to do the right things. He hopes that we will be kind and good because we want to. And God will help us do the right things if we ask him. But Pilate didn't ask him.

Yet Jesus loved Pilate too and wanted to give him a chance to be in his kingdom. Maybe Pilate didn't understand. But he did agree that Jesus was a good man.

Bible reading: John 18:33-38

What question from Pilate did Jesus answer? Why do you think Jesus talked with Pilate? How did Pilate's attitude change after talking with Jesus?

We thank you, Jesus, that you are concerned to have each one of us in your kingdom. Amen.

A verse to remember:

"For this I have come into the world, to bear witness to the truth" (John 18:37).

62

Has anyone ever taken your place so you didn't have to go through something that you knew would be unpleasant?

PILATE GUESSED WRONG

Pilate, the military judge, thought he had figured out a way to let Jesus go free. He knew the enemies of Jesus could make trouble for him, so he didn't want to displease them. But he also knew it would not be right to have Jesus killed, because Jesus had done nothing wrong.

So he announced to the people, "This weekend is the holiday when I always let one prisoner out of jail. Do you want him to be Barabbas or Jesus this year?" Everyone knew about Barabbas. He was guilty of terrible crimes. Surely, Pilate thought, the people won't want him loose.

But Pilate guessed wrong. The enemies of Jesus got the people to shout that they wanted Barabbas. This wasn't the way Pilate had planned it. The people kept

shouting, "Give us Barabbas!" until Pilate finally sent word to the prison to let Barabbas out. Jesus remained a prisoner.

The people did not care what happened to Barabbas. They just wanted to get rid of Jesus. Jesus cared for Barabbas more than they did. No doubt Jesus was happy he could save Barabbas' life. That's why he came to earth—to save the lives of all of us.

When the jailer unlocked the door of his cell and said, "Okay, you can go now," Barabbas may have thought someone was playing a trick on him. You didn't often get out of jail in those days. But it wasn't a trick. He was free because of Jesus.

We don't know what happened to Barabbas or what he thought of the one who took his place in jail. But we do know that in a very real way, Jesus has taken our place too. He died on the cross so we would not have to die for our sins. He sets us free when we have deserved to be punished for doing wrong.

Bible reading: Matthew 27:15-22

Why did Pilate offer the people a choice of who should be set free? Why did they choose Barabbas? In what way has Jesus taken our place?

Dear Lord Jesus, we thank you that you have suffered and died in our place. Help us to live in your family. Amen.

Something to do:

Think of a way you can take someone's place (perhaps your secret friend) by doing something for him or her, especially something that would be hard or unpleasant.

GAMES

How would you act if you met a king?

For some of the soldiers, the trial and sentencing of Jesus was like a game. At least they made a game out of it.

During the trial they heard Jesus called a prophet. So they put a blindfold on him, then hit him and asked, "Which one of us hit you that time? If you are a prophet you should be able to tell."

Later they heard someone call Jesus a king. So they decided to dress him up to imitate a king. They got a purple coat and threw it over him, pretending it was a royal robe. They gave him a cat-tail to hold. This was supposed to take the place of a jeweled cane that kings hold to show they have power. Cruelest of all they made a crown for him. It was made of sharp thorns that cut into his head.

The soldiers were being cruel, but not because they had anything against Jesus. They didn't know

how kind he was; they didn't know much about him. They couldn't have guessed that he really was a king, king of all the world. No doubt they would have treated him differently if they had known. But after all, the religious leaders were cruel to Jesus too, and the soldiers just followed their example.

There are still people who treat Jesus as though he were part of a game, although not always in as cruel a way. Some people may call Jesus a king, but they're only fooling. They don't serve him or obey him or honor him as they would a real king. They may call him a prophet, but they pay little attention to what he tells them.

Such attitudes by people today make Jesus just as unhappy as the cruel treatment he got from the soldiers. For the soldiers may not have known any better. But we do. We know that Jesus is not just a make-believe king. And we can show that we believe Jesus is our king by the way we serve him.

Bible reading: Mark 15:16-20

Why did the soldiers make fun of Jesus? How might people make fun of Jesus today? How will we act if we really believe Jesus is our king?

Jesus, we don't ever want to make fun of you. Keep us from doing it. And thank you for being our king. Amen.

Something to do:

Make something—a symbol, picture, sculpture, poster — to show how you feel about Jesus being your king.

KING ON A CROSS

What do you think of when you hear the word "king"?

Kings usually live in fine palaces and ride in fine cars. They wear expensive clothes. They have many servants who are ready to do anything that is asked of them.

Therefore it must have seemed odd to people walking by on the road to see the sign on the cross over Jesus. For the sign read: "Jesus of Nazareth, the King of the Jews."

That man was a king? He surely didn't look like one. He had no clothes, no friends or servants who could help him; he was dying as an unwanted criminal. What kind of a king was that?

Pilate put up the sign. When some of the people saw it they complained that it was an insult to them to call such a person their king. "Change your sign," they demanded, "to read, 'He said he was a king.'" Pilate refused. "It stays just the way I wrote it," he said.

Maybe he wanted to insult the leaders of the people because they had put him in a position where he felt he had to sentence Jesus to death whether he wanted to or not. Or maybe he felt Jesus really was a king. When Jesus had talked about his kingdom and how it was concerned with truth, Pilate seemed to be impressed. But we don't know what he really thought.

We do know that it isn't how a person looks that makes him a king. It is rather who he is and what he is able to do. On the cross Jesus looked less like a king than anyone. Yet he is the greatest king there is. He is not concerned with palaces and jewelry and other finery that we think about in connection with kings. He's concerned about the people in his kingdom and what he can do for them. He wants them all to know what is true and right. He wants them all to live in love and peace.

Bible reading: John 19:17-22

Who put up the sign that called Jesus a king? What did some of the people say about it? How can we be in Jesus' kingdom?

We're glad you are a king, Jesus, king of all the world. We want to serve you always. Amen.

A verse to remember:

"He is Lord of lords, and King of kings" (Rev. 17:14).

FORGIVEN

When was the last time you heard someone say the words, "I forgive you"?

When we are in trouble or are hurt, we think about ourselves. We are concerned with how we can stop the pain or how we can stick it out in some, way.

Jesus was different. Even when he was suffering the worst pain we can imagine, he was thinking about other people and what he could do for them. After he had been nailed to the cross, instead of crying out in pain, or thinking about how badly he had been treated, he prayed for those who were hurting him.

"Father, forgive them," he prayed. No doubt he was thinking of the Roman soldiers who had put him on the cross. But he probably meant also the people who had worked to get him sentenced to death. He loved them all.

We too are included in his prayer. The things we do wrong

need to be forgiven too. "Father, forgive them," applies to our sinfulness today, just as it did to those who put Jesus to death.

Jesus offered forgiveness before anyone asked for it. Maybe many of the people who caused him to be crucified never even felt sorry for what they did. Jesus died in order to be able to forgive the sins of everyone—even those who never ask for it.

When someone asks us to forgive him for doing something wrong, we often say something like, "That's all right," or "It doesn't make any difference." And usually that is true. So many of the wrongs that are done against us don't have any lasting effect. Next year we will have forgotten all about it.

But Jesus didn't say that it was all right that people were hurting him. He couldn't. For what they were doing did matter. It caused his death. But the great thing about the love of Jesus is that although our sins matter a great deal to him, he still says, "I forgive." He says it to all of us.

Bible reading: Luke 23:33-37

Why wouldn't you expect Jesus to pray for forgiveness for others at this time? Who do you think is included in his prayer? How should we let people know we forgive them if they have done something against us?

We thank you, Jesus, that you are willing to forgive our sins. Help us to be willing to forgive others. Amen.

Something to do:

If someone you know—a member of your family or a friend—has done something against you, tell that person you forgive him or her. If you have done something wrong to someone else, ask that person to forgive you.

72

When a person is being treated badly, do you think he is likely to be kind or mean to other people?

TWO ROBBERS

While Jesus was hanging on the cross, some of the people standing nearby kept on teasing him. "If you're really a king," they shouted at him, "why don't you come down from the cross? Then we'll believe you." Then they laughed.

Two robbers were crucified at the same time as Jesus. One of them joined in the teasing. "Didn't you say you were somebody great?" he said. "Why don't you save yourself? And while you're at it, take us along." Maybe he thought he could take his mind off his own pain by making Jesus feel worse.

But the other robber told him to stop. "We at least know we had this punishment coming to us," he said. "But this man hasn't done anything wrong." Then he turned to Jesus and said, "Remember me,

Jesus, when you take over in your kingdom."

Again Jesus showed how much he loves people and wants to help those in need, no matter who they are. To the second robber he said, "I promise you that today you'll be with me in paradise." Jesus loved the robber and was dying for him too. It must have helped that man to know that even after his wicked life there was hope for him. God loved him and was going to make room for him in heaven right away.

Those words of Jesus have meant much to Christians ever since. They give us something great to look forward to. Jesus promises that we shall share his glorious future with him. For us it won't be today. But we know that someday we too shall be with him in paradise.

Bible reading: Luke 23:39-43

How did the two robbers differ in the way they talked to Jesus? What promise did Jesus give? What does paradise mean to you?

We thank you, Jesus, that we can look forward to being with you forever in paradise. Amen.

A verse to remember:

"Today you will be with me in paradise" (Luke 23:43).

How long should a child honor his father and mother?

MOTHER

Mary, the mother of Jesus, was standing near the cross as Jesus hung on it. Now she understood the strange words someone had said to her when Jesus was born: that sorrow would break her heart because of her son. It wasn't any easier for Mary than for anyone else to understand why Jesus should be put to death.

She did know that she was losing her oldest son. And she was losing him in a terrible way; he was being killed as a criminal by the government. Perhaps worst of all, there was nothing she could do for him.

But Jesus could still do something for her. And he did. He knew there would be an empty spot in her life after he was gone. So he gave her someone to take his place: his disciple John. "Here is a son to take my place," he said to her, meaning John, who was nearby.

Then to John he said, "From now on, she is your mother." And from that time on John provided a home for Mary, just as Jesus would have done.

Again it is surprising that Jesus could think of anyone else while he was suffering on the cross. Yet even when he was going through torture, he made sure to take care of his responsibility to his mother. He took seriously the commandment, "Honor your father and mother."

Some people seem to think parents are only to help them; they may honor them during the years when they are small children, living at home; but after they grow older and move away they forget them. Jesus gave us an example to follow. He honored his parents after he was a grown man. He cared for them as long as they lived. He provided for his mother when she was old as she had taken care of him when he was young.

Bible reading: John 19:25-27

Who did Jesus say should take his place in his mother's family? What did he mean when he told John that Mary was his mother? How can we honor our parents now? When we are grown up?

We thank you for our mothers, Father in heaven. Help us to remember what they have done for us and to honor them all our life. Amen.

Something to do:

Do something special to show your mother how much you love her.

ALONE

When have you felt the most lonely?

To be lonely is a sad feeling. Sometimes we feel lonely when we are all by ourselves, and don't want to be. Maybe we are alone in an empty house; or walking down a dark street where we can see no one else. How we wait for another person to show up; almost anyone will do.

At other times we are lonely even though other people are near. We may be in a strange place where there are many people but no one we know. It could be the first day of school; or a crowded city street. Until we get to know these people around us and they begin to pay some attention to us, we can be very lonely.

We may also feel alone if we are afraid or facing something unpleasant and no one is nearby to help. Maybe you've been called into the principal's office because of some mischief. Other people are there,

78

but you feel all alone. Or you might feel lonely while waiting in a doctor's or dentist's office.

Jesus knew what it means to be lonely. Sometimes he went off by himself. But he wasn't lonely then, for he was talking to his Heavenly Father. At other times he may have felt lonely because he didn't really have a place to call home. But the only time he said he was lonely was while he was on the cross. Even though friends stood near by, they couldn't help him. He was particularly lonely because he felt he could not get in touch with God. "My God, my God," he cried, "why have you left me all alone?" He had to go through this suffering and death all by himself.

We've never had to be that lonely. For even if everybody else is gone, God has never left us. Ever since the day we were born, God has been near us. He loves us and wants to help us. We don't ever have to feel lonely. Jesus was lonely so we wouldn't have to be.

Bible reading: Matthew 27:45-49

What makes a person feel lonely? Where did Jesus feel most alone? Why? What should we do when we feel lonely?

Thank you, Jesus, for always being with us. Help us to think of you when we feel lonely. Amen.

Something to do:

Think of someone who may be lonely. Decide on something you can do to make him or her feel less lonely.

79

Think of the time you were the thirstiest you've ever been. What did you do about it?

THIRSTY

Everyone knows what it is to be thirsty. Usually it happens at the worst possible times. We don't want it that way, but it just happens, and we can't help it. Maybe it's in the middle of the night when everyone is asleep. Or maybe you're in the middle of a field on a hot day and water is a long way off. Perhaps it happens during a long trip in the car, usually just after you've stopped—but you weren't thirsty then.

If we had to go without water for a long enough time, we would die. But it rarely is that serious when we're thirsty. We can get something to drink by hollering for our parents, or walking to the edge of the field, or driving off the freeway. But the fact that our life isn't in danger, that water is fairly close at hand, that by a little effort we can get a drink doesn't take

away that feeling of thirst. It's uncomfortable, it makes us irritable, and we insist that something be done about it.

Does it surprise us to think of Jesus as being thirsty? And of all the bad places it could happen, it was while he was on the cross. Jesus spoke only seven times from the cross. But one of those sentences was, "I'm thirsty."

Whatever else this means, it shows us how human Jesus was. He also had some of our strange weaknesses, like getting thirsty in the worst possible times and places. It tells us too that he knows what we go through; he has suffered everything we suffer. He knows why we sometimes feel cross or tired or gloomy. He understands why we call for Dad at night just because we're thirsty.

So when we are thirsty, or have any other problem, we can remember that Jesus often felt this way too. And he wants to help us in the big and little problems of life.

Bible reading: John 19:28-29

Where was Jesus when he said he was thirsty? What does this tell you about Jesus? How does it help you to know that Jesus was thirsty?

Jesus, we're glad you understand the things that cause us problems and cause us to be problems to others. Help us to overcome our problems in the best way. Amen.

Something to do:

Many people are thirsty and hungry in the world because they haven't enough money to buy the food they need. Decide what you can do to help them.

FINISHED

Think of the best job you ever did. Would you say it was perfect?

Only one person in all the world's history could honestly say when he came to the end of his life, "I've done everything I should have done, and done it perfectly." That person was Jesus.

Many people have lived much longer. Many have ruled large countries, written hundreds of books, won mighty battles, invented wonderful machines, built magnificent buildings. Jesus did none of these things. Yet the people who have done such things could not honestly say they had done everything they should have; nor that what they had done was perfect.

Jesus had a short life, only about 33 years. In just three of those years he did the job he came to this world to do. Yet what he did is more important to the people of the world than everything all the great men who have ever lived have done.

For Jesus affected not only our life here on earth—showing us how our lives can be more worthwhile for ourselves and others. He has also told us that we can live with him in heaven forever. He made it possible by the job he finished here on earth. He did it perfectly. He did it by living a perfect life, and by giving up that life for us. This was the only way he could take away our sin so that he could bring us to heaven with him.

Since Jesus had done what he came to do, his life could end. In fact, it was in dying that he completed his work.

"It is finished," he said. Not just his life on earth. But the job he came to do. Because of this, our sins have been forgiven and we can live with him forever.

Bible reading: John 19:30

How was Jesus able to finish his work in such a short time? What had Jesus finished? What difference does it make to us?

Thank you, Jesus, for finishing your work so perfectly. Amen.

A verse to remember:

"It is finished" (John 19:30).

How do you feel when you are about to do something so new or different that you're not sure how it's going to turn out?

INTO THE UNKNOWN

Many children when they go to bed say the prayer, "Now I lay me down to sleep, I pray the Lord my soul to keep." When they do so, they are praying a prayer very much like one that Jesus prayed on the cross.

Jesus had finished the work he came to do. He was ready to die. Yet it was as hard for him to give up his life as it is for any person. He was going into the unknown—he had never died before. It must have made him somewhat uneasy. So he turned his life over to God for safekeeping.

"Father," he prayed, "I am putting my life into your hands." Those were the last words he said before he died.

Those words tell us how Jesus lived his whole life. Everything he did was according to what his

85

Father wanted. He trusted the Father to take care of everything that happened. Now when he had completed his work, he again trusted his future to the Father. He was sure that the Father would take care of him. So he left everything in God's hands.

Jesus gives us the faith to follow his example. There will be many times in our lives when we won't be exactly sure of what will happen. We may be worried about how things will come out. At such times we can safely say to God, "I'm leaving it in your hands." For God has told us in many ways that he will care for us. He can care for us much better than we can ourselves.

When we see how God cares for us through everything that happens in our life, we can be sure he will care for us when we die too. We don't look forward to dying. We don't know what it will be like. But we can be sure that when we are with God it will be all right.

Bible reading: Luke 23:44-46

What were Jesus' last words before he died? What did he expect his Father to do? When would it be good for us to pray a similar prayer?

Father, there are many times when we don't know how things will turn out. Take care of us then, as you always do. Amen.

Something to do:

Think of something coming up that you are a little worried about. Make up a prayer asking God to take care of it.

WHEN BAD IS GOOD

Can you think of any reason why we call the day Jesus died *Good* Friday?

We don't like to think of Jesus dying, and it makes us sad to remember what happened on the first Good Friday. Some people call it Black Friday or Long Friday instead of Good Friday. The Bible tells us there was a strange darkness while Jesus was on the cross, as though the sun didn't want to shine on such a terrible deed. When Jesus died there was an earthquake as if the world itself were shuddering because of what was happening. It seemed that death and evil had won a great victory, even over Jesus.

But God wasn't through yet. He was going to show everyone that his power is stronger than the power of death. He was going to show us that something good can come out of what looks like the worst possible situation.

A little girl once asked her

mother why she had such terrible scars on her arms. She didn't even want to look at them because they were so ugly. Her mother replied that once the little girl had fallen into a fire. In trying to rescue her, the mother had been badly burned, but she saved the little girl's life. When the girl heard that she said, "Now those scars aren't ugly, because I know they show how much you love me."

That's the way we feel about Good Friday. We're sorry that Jesus had to suffer and die, but we love him for doing it to save us. It's a Good Friday because on this day Jesus took our sins away so we can live with him forever.

Bible reading:

Matthew 27:50-53

What strange things happened on Good Friday? Why is Good Friday a sad day? Why can we still call it good?

As we remember how you suffered and died, Jesus, we are sorry. But we are thankful that because of what you went through we can live with you forever. Amen.

Something to do:

Discuss what might be a good way to observe Good Friday. Plan what you will do on Good Friday in memory of what Jesus has done.

A
CONVINCED
SOLDIER

What impresses you most from what you know about Jesus?

Roman soldiers had the job of putting Jesus on the cross. They also had to stand guard while he hung there.

Some of them probably didn't care for the job, but they had to do it. Others divided up Jesus' clothes for themselves and even threw dice to decide who should get his best piece of clothing—a cloak.

Not all of the soldiers made fun of Jesus or were cruel to him. Most of them probably didn't think much about him one way or the other. They may have seen so many crucifixions that they didn't think much of it any more.

But the soldier in charge, called a centurion, paid close attention to everything that went on. He had to make sure nothing went wrong.

When Jesus finally died, this centurion said, "This man must have been a son of God." As far as we know, that soldier had never seen

Jesus before. What do you suppose impressed him so much about Jesus?

Was it the quiet way he accepted what came, not arguing with the judge and not fighting the soldiers —not crying out in anger or pain? Was it the way he showed his love for others, even while on the cross: for his mother—for the robber—for those who were killing him? Had the centurion heard something Jesus said during his ministry? Had he talked to the friends of Jesus and learned what kind of a man he was? Was it the final words, when Jesus said "It is finished," and handed over his life to his Father?

We have no way of knowing. But in just a few hours, the centurion saw enough of Jesus to conclude that he must be a son of God.

We have a much better chance to learn about Jesus—from our parents and teachers; from our church; from our Bible. And it leads us to say too, "Jesus is the Son of God."

Bible reading: Mark 15:37-39

What did the centurion say about Jesus? From what you have learned about Jesus, what would you add to what the centurion said?

We praise you, Jesus. You are the Son of God and our Savior. Amen.

Something to do:

The cross is used as a symbol to remind us of what Jesus went through for us. Using this symbol, make something, such as a wooden or metal cross, a picture or poster, to remind you of Jesus' love.

91

OUT OF THE GROUND

We almost always have funerals after people have died. What good do you think they do?

There wasn't time for a funeral after Jesus died, because he had to be buried before the Sabbath began at sundown. So he was buried quickly by some friends who asked Pilate for permission to take him from the cross.

A rich man named Joseph of Arimathea thought a great deal of Jesus and decided he wanted to take care of burying his body. Like many people today, he had prepared a place for himself to be buried. In those days in Palestine people were often buried in caves rather than in the ground. Joseph had cut out a large hole in the side of a rocky cliff as a grave. It was near the place where Jesus was crucified. To this grave Joseph took the body of Jesus to be buried.

Most people don't like funerals. And if Jesus' body had stayed in that hole in the rock, funerals

would always be terribly sad and nothing else. But we know that Jesus didn't stay in that grave. He came out alive. And because he came to life again he has promised that we too can come to life after we die and go to live with him.

For those who love Jesus, funerals are no longer quite as sad as they would be otherwise. We are still sad when we lose a friend who dies. But because Jesus died and came to life again, we know our friends who believed in him will rise too.

Jesus once said that dying, for those who believe in him, is something like planting a seed. The seed dies, but a plant comes from it. Because of Jesus, when we die believing in him we will live again.

Bible reading: Mark 15:42-46

Who took care of the burial of Jesus? What kind of a grave did Jesus have? Why are burials not as sad for us as they would be if Jesus hadn't been buried?

We thank you, Jesus, that although you were buried, you came to life again. Help us to believe that you will raise us, too. Amen.

Something to do:

A plant growing out of the ground is sometimes used as a symbol of Jesus coming out of the grave. So is a butterfly that comes out of its cocoon. Can you think of other similar examples? Make a drawing or poster of a symbol of the resurrection.

THE BEST NEWS

Why is Easter different from other Sundays?

Many Christians like to get up very early on Easter Sunday. Maybe it's because they want to hear the good news of Easter as early in the day as possible. For it is the best news people in the world have ever heard.

Or maybe it is because the first time this news was announced was very early in the morning. Even before the sun had come up, Mary the mother of Jesus and two other women went to the place where Jesus had been buried. They felt that because of the rush to bury him before the Sabbath he hadn't been given a proper funeral. They wanted to show their love and respect for him by trying to do something more, even after he had been put in the grave.

But when they came to Joseph's tomb they found the large rock that had closed the opening was pushed away. The grave was open.

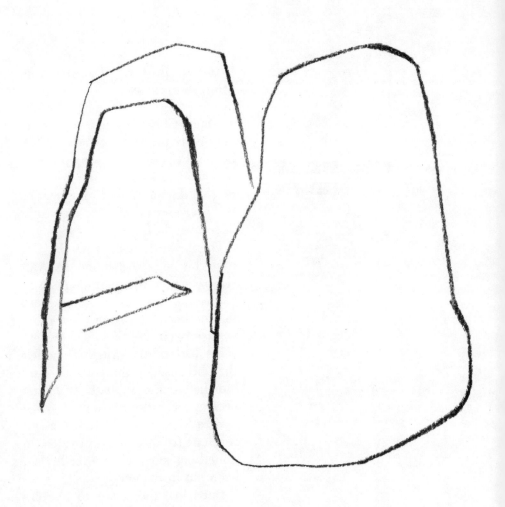

They began to be afraid that something terrible had happened. When they were close enough they could see that nothing was in the hole in the rock. The body of Jesus wasn't there.

They did see a strange man, however. They realized he must be an angel. "Don't be surprised," he said. "You're looking for Jesus of Nazareth. He has risen. He is not here. See, the grave is empty. Go and tell his disciples."

That was the best news anyone ever heard. Not even death could stop Jesus. He was alive! That's why we celebrate Easter. That's why we celebrate every Sunday by going to church. Jesus lives!

Bible reading: Mark 16:1-7

What did the women find at the tomb? What did they hear? Why was this good news to them? To us?

Father, we are happy because of what happened that first Easter. We praise you for the good news that Jesus rose. We praise you for the forgiveness of sins Jesus won for us and the hope we now have of living with you forever. Amen.

A verse to remember:

"He has risen, he is not here" (Mark 16:6).

Try to imagine what you would have thought if you had been a disciple and heard the news that Jesus' body was not in the grave.

EMPTY

John reached the tomb of Jesus on Easter morning before Peter. John was younger; he could run faster. When these two disciples heard the news that Jesus was not in the grave where he had been buried, they both ran as fast as they could to the garden where the grave was. As they ran they must have been wondering what terrible thing had happened.

When John got there, he stopped at the entrance of the tomb. He stooped down and looked inside. It was true; there was no body.

Then Peter came puffing up. He didn't stop at the entrance; he went right into the cave. There he saw a strange thing. The long cloth in which Jesus had been wrapped for burial was lying there. Another

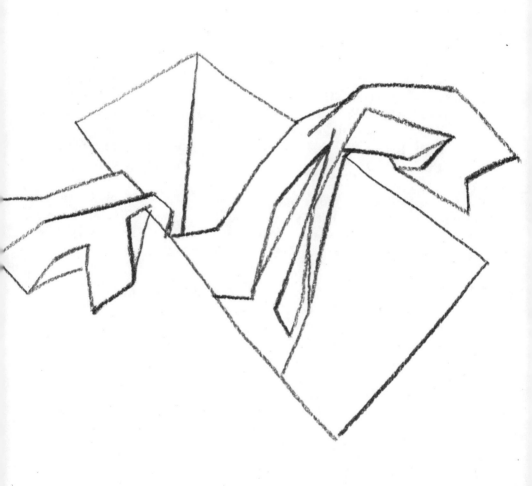

cloth that had been around his head was rolled up by itself.

John followed Peter into the tomb. When he saw these things he realized that what they had been afraid of hadn't happened. No one had come and stolen the body of Jesus. They wouldn't have left the wrappings like that. Whatever happened had been carefully done, not in a hurry.

What could it mean? Perhaps John remembered what Jesus had talked about so often those last few months. Finally it came to him. Jesus was alive again! He had come out of the grave alive, as he had said.

The empty tomb means that God has power even over death. And the same power of God that brought Jesus back to life, will one day bring us from death to life with God in heaven.

Bible reading: John 20:1-9

Why did the disciples run to the tomb? What did they see there? What was the meaning of what they saw in the tomb?

Jesus, we're so glad you were able to come to life and leave the grave, we don't know what to say. Thank you! Amen.

Something to do:

See how many hymns you can find that talk about Jesus rising from the dead. Sing one of them.

Have there been times when you didn't recognize someone because you didn't expect to see him?

UNEXPECTED

Mary Magdalene was the first person to see Jesus after he came out of the grave alive. At first she didn't know who he was. Jesus must have been changed in some way, because people didn't always recognize him. Or it may have been that they weren't expecting to see him.

Mary had been one of those who came early in the morning to the tomb of Jesus—and found it empty. After she had run to report this to the disciples, she returned to the grave. As she stood there, crying, she saw two angels in the tomb. "Lady, why are you crying?" they asked her.

"Because they have taken away my Lord, and I don't know where they put him," she replied through her tears.

She turned away and saw a man standing nearby. He too asked her, "Lady, why are you crying? Who are you looking for?"

She thought he was the caretaker of the garden. So she said to him, "Sir, if you took him away, tell me where you put him and I'll take care of him."

The man said one word, "Mary." At once she knew he was Jesus.

"My Master," she said, hardly believing it could be true.

Jesus told her that he was going to his Father, and that she should tell the disciples that he was alive. Happily she went on her way to tell them that she had seen Jesus.

Many people today know something about Jesus. But like Mary, they don't really recognize who he is. Not until they become aware that he is their Savior, who knows and calls them by name, do they come to believe in him. For he is not just another person in history. He is our teacher, our Savior, our God.

Bible reading: John 20:11-18

Why was Mary crying? Who did she see? How did she come to recognize Jesus?

We thank you, Jesus, that you know us by our own names, and that you want to be our Savior. Amen.

A verse to remember:

"(He) desires all men to be saved and to come to the knowledge of the truth" (1 Timothy 2:4).

TOO GOOD
TO
BE TRUE

Have you ever heard anything "too good to be true"? Did you believe it anyway?

Easter Sunday afternoon two disciples were walking from Jerusalem to a village called Emmaus. As they walked they talked about what had happened to Jesus; how he had been arrested, sentenced, and crucified. You could tell how discouraged they were by their sad faces and sorrowful voices. They had believed so strongly that Jesus was the leader God had promised. Now they had lost all hope and didn't know what to do.

They were so busy talking that they didn't notice a man come up alongside them. "What are you talking about that makes you so sad?" he asked.

"You must be the only person in Jerusalem who doesn't know what's happened," they answered.

"What?" the man asked.

They began to tell him about Jesus—that he had been a great

teacher who did miracles and they had hoped he was the one who would deliver their nation. But their hopes had been dashed when the leaders of the nation had him put to death as a criminal.

They also mentioned that the body had disappeared from the grave, and that some claimed they had seen angels who said Jesus was alive. But they didn't believe it; it was too good to be true.

Then the stranger began explaining to them what kind of a Savior the Old Testament had promised. The things that had just happened were necessary, he said, for this was how the Savior was to do what God wanted.

When they reached Emmaus, the couple invited their companion to have supper with them. At the table this man took the bread and gave a blessing—and it struck the other two that this was how Jesus used to do it. And suddenly they realized, it was Jesus! Then all at once he was gone.

They were so excited that they left their supper and went back to Jerusalem to tell the other disciples that they had seen Jesus. He was alive! This news was too good to keep to themselves.

Bible reading: Luke 24:13-35

Why did the disciples not believe Jesus was alive? What did Jesus tell the two disciples on the road? What caused them to recognize Jesus?

Help us, Jesus, not to be discouraged by our troubles so that we don't realize when you are with us. Teach us to understand what you have done and are doing for us. Amen.

Something to do:

Make a list of things in your daily life that remind you that Jesus came to life again.

105

What would you think if someone suddenly appeared in your
room without coming through
the door?

BEHIND LOCKED DOORS

After Jesus had been crucified,
the disciples were afraid that the
rulers would try to seize anyone
who had been with Jesus. They
tried to stay off the streets and do
nothing that would cause people to
notice them. Even the news that
Jesus was alive again didn't take
away their fear. The evening of
Easter day they were together in
someone's house. They made sure
the doors were locked. Probably
they were talking about what had
happened and what they should
do next.

Suddenly Jesus was there with
them. He hadn't opened the door;
he was just there. Locked doors
don't stop Jesus any more than a
sealed grave could.

Instead of being happy to see
him, the disciples were frightened.

They thought he was a ghost and no longer a real person.

"Why are you so scared?" Jesus asked them. "What are you wondering about? Look at me carefully to see that it is I. You can touch me to make sure, for a ghost doesn't have hands and feet as I do."

The disciples were glad to hear Jesus speak. But they still didn't know what to think.

So Jesus asked them, "Do you have anything here to eat?" They gave him a piece of fish left over from supper and he ate it in front of them. Ghosts don't eat food. It had to be Jesus—alive.

Then Jesus began to explain that his suffering and death had been a part of God's plan and that the Old Testament had told about it. All he went through was necessary so the sins of people could be forgiven. And now, he said, they had a job—to get out from behind the locked doors and tell this news to everybody.

Bible reading: Luke 24:36-47

Why did the disciples think Jesus was a ghost? What did he do to convince them he wasn't? What job did Jesus have for them to do?

Forgive us, Jesus, for ever being scared of what other people think of us for being your followers. Help us to be brave enough to tell others what you have done for us. Amen.

Something to do:

Watch a TV program to see if anyone is afraid to do what he knows is right. Talk about how things might have been different if he had done what he knew he should do.

How do *you* know Jesus rose from death?

PROOF

Some people always seem to be away just when the most interesting things are going on. They miss out on all the excitement. Thomas may have been such a person.

He was absent when Jesus came to see the apostles on the evening of Easter Sunday. When they excitedly told him what he had missed, he thought they must be out of their minds. People don't suddenly appear in a room with the doors all closed, as they said Jesus had done.

"I don't believe it," he said. "You must have been seeing things. You were so upset by what's happened the last few days that you imagined you saw Jesus. Unless I get some real proof—unless I can see the sores in Jesus' body and touch the holes made by the nails when he was crucified, I'm not going to be fooled into thinking he's alive."

Jesus doesn't give up on those

who have a hard time believing, like Thomas. He loves them as much as anyone else, and does what he can to help them believe.

So a week later Jesus came to the disciples again. This time Thomas was there. Again the doors were carefully closed and locked. And again Jesus suddenly stood in the room with them. He spoke especially to Thomas. "Go ahead and put your finger in the sores on my hands and feet," he told him. "I want you to believe."

But Thomas no longer had to have that kind of proof that Jesus was alive. When he saw Jesus, it was enough for him. "My Lord and my God," he cried out to Jesus.

"You have believed after seeing me," Jesus answered. "Others will believe who haven't seen me—they too will be blessed."

Bible reading: John 20:24-29

Who didn't believe Jesus was alive? Why? What convinced him? What can we do for someone who doesn't believe that Jesus is alive?

Thank you, Jesus, for helping us to believe in you. Help us to know that you are here with us, even if we can't see you. Amen.

A verse to remember:

"Believe in the Lord Jesus, and you will be saved" (Acts 16:31).

A TIME TO PRAISE

Can you think of any words from a foreign language that you use in your church services?

We often sing hymns and songs that contain the word "alleluia" (also spelled "hallelujah"). Do you know what it means?

This word is used especially at Easter time. It is the Hebrew way of saying "praise the Lord." Surely there is no time when we feel more like praising God than at Easter. Then as at no other time we are reminded of God's power and how he has used this power for us. When we have heard once again the news that Jesus has risen from death, it is only natural that we would want to thank God and tell everyone how great he is. And that's part of what it means to praise him.

The news of Easter tells us that God is more powerful than anyone or anything; he has defeated the devil; he has forgiven our sins; he has made it possible for us

111

to live in heaven with him. Alleluia! Praise the Lord!

We use the word in many songs and also at other times in our worship services. Often the congregation sings "Alleluia" as a response.

In the picture of heaven given in the Book of Revelation, the people there often use the word "alleluia" to show how happy they are, and to praise God: "Hallelujah! Salvation and glory and power belong to our God . . . Hallelujah! For the Lord our God the Almighty reigns," they say (Rev. 19). Several psalms begin and end with Hallelujah: Praise the Lord!

Bible reading: Psalm 150

What does "alleluia" mean? Why is it especially used at Easter time? What does it mean to praise God? How can we praise him?

Dear God, we say Alleluia, Praise the Lord, for the great things you have done for us. Amen.

Something to do:

Make a list of other foreign words you use in church and learn their meaning.

ADVANCE AGENT

If you were going to arrange a trip for someone, what things would you be concerned about?

When presidents and kings and other famous people go on a trip, someone called an advance agent always goes ahead of them. His job is to make sure that everything is ready. He inspects the airplane and checks on arrangements at the airports. He places guards to protect him and orders a big car to take the person from the airport to the hotel. He looks over the hotel room and asks what will be served at meals. He makes out a schedule and insists that everyone who has anything to do with the trip is on hand at the right time and place so everything can go smoothly.

Most of us have no advance agent when we go on a trip; we make our own arrangements. Sometimes we may phone ahead for a reservation; then we at least know a place will be ready for us when

114

we get there. Otherwise we take our chances and never are quite sure what we'll find.

Jesus treats us as though we were presidents or kings. He goes ahead of us himself, like an advance agent, to make sure everything is ready for us in his kingdom. He personally is making all the arrangements for all that we will need. When he left this earth he said he was going to make things ready for us in God's house. We don't have to worry that there won't be enough room. "My father's house has many rooms," he said.

Jesus also promises that when he has everything ready, he'll come back for us so we can go and live with him in heaven. In the meantime, he's told us what to do to be sure we'll end up in the Father's house. That way is to believe in Jesus.

Sometimes we talk about death as a long journey. When we go on that long journey, we can be sure that Jesus will go with us. He has gone there ahead of us to get everything ready as he waits to guide us to heaven where we can live forever with him.

Bible reading: John 14:1-6

What did Jesus say he was going to do when he left this world? How can we be sure of getting to heaven?

Lord Jesus, thank you for getting everything ready for us. Help us to keep believing in you so you can bring us into the home you've made ready for us in heaven. Amen.

A verse to remember:

"I am the way, and the truth, and the life" (John 14:6).

Can you think of some times when you felt Jesus was with you, helping you in a special way?

TOGETHER

Jesus promised that he would always be with us, even after he left this world. How does he keep this promise?

One of the ways is through the church. The Bible calls Jesus the head of the church. As members of the church, we are like parts of his body. We are a part of him, doing his work, living and growing with him. When we're with the church, that is, with other people who believe in Jesus, then we're with him.

Another way is through the Bible. In the Bible we have Jesus' words, and other things God wants us to know. These words have been written in a book to help us. When we read in our Bible about God's love for us we can hear Jesus speaking to us. When we pay attention to his words, Jesus is with us.

116

A third way is through prayer. Jesus often told us to pray. He promised many times that God would hear and answer our prayers. By praying, Christians can talk with God even if they can't see him. They know he is listening as he promised he would, and that he will answer—not in words, perhaps, but in some way.

We are also with Jesus when we do the work he wants us to do, helping people. He is there working with us. He said that when we help someone in need we are really helping him.

We want to be with Jesus as much as possible. These are some of the ways he is with us today.

Bible reading: Matthew 28:18-20

What are some ways we can be with Jesus today? Which way do you like best?

Keep us near you, Jesus, at all times. Help us to hear you speaking to us in your Word, and to work with you in helping people. Amen.

A verse to remember:

"I am with you always" (Matt. 28:20).

A SUPPER TO REMEMBER

When are Communion services held in your church?

Christians go to Communion, or the Lord's Supper, because Jesus himself asked us to do it. He said we should do it to remember him.

Would we forget Jesus without these special services? No, that isn't likely. But these services can make him seem closer to us—more real—actually with us.

If we never spend any time with a person who is our best friend, it isn't long before he isn't our best friend any more. We want to be with those we love. And in Communion Jesus is with us in a special way.

And though we wouldn't forget about Jesus altogether, we might begin to think less about what is most important about him and what he did for us. There are people who know that Jesus was a fine man and a great teacher and healer. But they seem to have forgotten that he is a Savior who for-

gives us all our sins. Or they don't think of him as the Lord whom they wish to serve.

Jesus gave us what we call the Lord's Supper to help us remember and believe that he forgives us. It should therefore be a happy time. In Communion Jesus comes to us in a special way, though we can't understand it exactly. As the minister gives bread (or wafers) and wine to us, we remember that Jesus gave his life for us. He did it, as he told us to remember, for the forgiveness of our sins.

So whenever we go to Communion, Jesus comes to us in a special way. And we are glad as we remember how he showed his love for us, giving his life to forgive us.

Bible reading:

1 Corinthians 11:23-26

Why does the church have Communion services? What good do they do? Who do you think should go to Communion?

We thank you, Jesus, that you came to give your life to forgive our sins. Help us to remember at all times how much you have done for us. Amen.

A verse to remember:

"Do this in remembrance of me" (1 Cor. 11:24).

FORTY DAYS

Can you remember what happened forty days ago?

Forty days may sound like a long time. But when it is all the time you have to be with someone you love very much, it is a very short time indeed.

Jesus stayed on earth with his disciples for forty days after his resurrection. It must have seemed like a very short time to him. For he knew that when the forty days were up he would be leaving them.

He would also be leaving the work he had started of telling the whole world about God's love. During his short life he had reached only a few of the people in the world. Now he was going to turn this job over to his followers. There was so much to tell them so they would be prepared for what they were to do. He couldn't possibly cover everything in forty days. Even if he could, they would be sure to forget much of it. And some of the things they wouldn't

121

understand till they were faced with certain problems.

So Jesus arranged for the training to continue after he left. He promised that the Holy Spirit would come to take his place. The Spirit would continue teaching the disciples to do the work Jesus had started. By promising to send someone to take his place Jesus also cheered up his followers who were sad that he would no longer be with them as he had been in the past.

Jesus promises the Holy Spirit to us too. For those of us who were alive when Jesus walked this earth it is an especially great promise. For the Holy Spirit carries on the work of Jesus in such a great way that at times it seems Jesus is right here with us.

The greatest gift we have is the Holy Spirit. Without him, we wouldn't know about Jesus or be able to believe in him. He is here with us now.

Bible reading: Acts 1:1-5

How long did Jesus stay on earth after his resurrection? What did he do during this time? How did he continue his work after he left the earth?

Thank you for sending the Holy Spirit to take your place, Jesus. Help us to listen to what he tells us. Amen.

Something to do:

For the next few days keep a record of the things you think the Holy Spirit is trying to teach you.

THE BEST REMINDER

When is the last time you forgot something you were supposed to remember?

How much can you remember from what you learned in school yesterday, or in Sunday school last Sunday, or from last week's sermon?

Sometimes we forget things because we weren't paying close enough attention, or because we didn't really understand what it was all about. Sometimes the one who is teaching or talking to us doesn't make it clear enough. But many more times we just plain forget.

The idea may seem clear to us when we hear it. We may agree that it is important. We may even say to ourselves, "I'm going to be sure to remember that." Yet before long it is completely out of our mind. Even tying a string around our finger doesn't always help us to remember.

Because this happens to all of

us, the Holy Spirit is a very valuable friend. For one of his jobs is to help us remember what Jesus has told us. Jesus said much that can help us when we have problems. But just when his words would be especially helpful for us we often can't remember them. The Holy Spirit will help us remember.

Not only does he prod our memories, but he continues to teach us, just as Jesus once did. He helps us to understand the Bible better when we read it, or he uses people he has taught earlier to explain things to us.

When Jesus promised to send the Holy Spirit he said he would teach us all things. That means he continues to teach us as long as we live.

Often we don't know what is the best thing to do. The Holy Spirit whom Jesus sent to us will teach us if we let him. He is the best teacher we could have.

Bible reading: John 14:25-27

What did Jesus say the Holy Spirit would do for us? Why is this work valuable? How does the Holy Spirit teach us the words of Jesus today?

There are many things to remember, Jesus. Help us to learn and remember what is most important. Amen.

Something to do:

One way to remember what Jesus said is to memorize parts of the Bible. List some verses you would like to memorize (beginning with some from this book), then begin to learn them. You may want to keep a chart, or make flash cards to help. (Some passages for starters might be Psalm 23, Matthew 5–7, or 1 Corinthians 13.)

WIND AND FIRE

How can you tell when a strong wind is blowing?

The sound of wind makes us all listen. It may cause us to act, too; to get into a house or behind a wall, or to close the windows, or to button up our coat.

Fire gets our attention too. Just about everybody seems to like to watch fire burn.

Isn't it strange that these two things, wind and fire, should be connected with the coming of the Holy Spirit whom Jesus promised to send? What do you suppose this means?

Jesus said that the Holy Spirit was like wind because no one can see wind, nor can we tell it where it should blow. But we can see where it has been. That's the way with the Holy Spirit. No one can see him, and we can't give the Holy Spirit orders as to where he should work or what he should do. But we can see where he has been working by

126

the changes that take place in people's lives.

Jesus might have added that wind can remind us of God's power too. Anyone who has been near a tornado or hurricane knows how much power the wind has. The Holy Spirit has more.

Fire also reminds us of the Holy Spirit. Fire makes things pure and clean. It burns waste. It separates metal, like iron, from ore. It provides warmth so we can live comfortably. It gives light. And if we don't respect it, it can destroy things.

The Holy Spirit does some things like that. He can cleanse us from sin. He can bring about a friendly feeling among people. He helps us to understand things.

Perhaps it isn't strange at all that fire and wind are connected with the coming of the Holy Spirit.

Bible reading: Acts 2:1-4

What were the signs of the coming of the Holy Spirit? How is the Holy Spirit like wind? How is he like fire?

Send your power and cleansing into our lives, O Holy Spirit. Amen.

Something to do:

Find a map and see how many of the countries mentioned in Acts 2:9-11 you can locate.

Can anyone in your family speak more than one language? What good is it to know more than one language?

A GOOD WIND

When the Holy Spirit came the first time, many people came running to see what the noise was all about. It sounded something like a tornado or hurricane.

These people happened to be from many different countries; they spoke many languages. It was important that the message about Jesus should get to their countries. Now of course God knows all the languages in the world. But he ordinarily depends on people to speak for him. And they don't always know the language of the person who needs to get God's message.

On Pentecost the Holy Spirit solved this problem by causing all of these people to hear what the disciples were saying in their own language. We don't know how he did this, whether he helped the disciples to speak these languages or whether the people just heard it this way. We do know that it helped to send God's message about Jesus and his love on its way to all the people of the world.

God's message is still being spread to many people who speak many different languages. But he uses a different method now. People who are going to bring the news of Jesus to someone who speaks a different language first study that language so they can speak it. Sometimes missionaries spend months or even years learning to speak a language.

Others spread God's message by translating the Bible. They write it in a new language so the people will be able to read about Jesus in words they can understand. Parts of the Bible have been printed in more than 1450 languages. The story of Jesus has been told in nearly every language there is. And God is pleased when we help to spread this message to people who have never heard it.

Bible reading: Acts 2:5-11

How did the news about Jesus get out to people of different countries on Pentecost? How does this message get out today? How can we help?

We thank you, Father, that you arranged to have the news about Jesus and his love brought to us in our language. Help those who are trying to bring it in more languages so that everybody in the world can know about Jesus. Amen.

Something to do:

Find out something about the work of the American Bible Society or some other group that brings the Bible to people in many languages. Your pastor can probably give you some information.

Do you know any person who is called a lord?

There aren't many lords around today. We hardly ever hear of them except in movies and stories about life hundreds of years ago. A few people in England are called lords, but the title doesn't mean nearly as much as it once did.

Years ago it was a great thing to be a lord. A lord was a person with a great deal of money and power. He ruled the people who lived on his land. He controlled their lives. He could decide what they did, how much they would get paid, where they could live—sometimes whether they lived or died.

When they called Jesus "Lord," the disciples probably were thinking about some of these powers of a lord. They meant to say that Jesus was their master in all ways. He controlled their lives. They were willing to let him decide what they should do.

LORD

When people had earthly lords they had no choice; if they lived in a certain place, a certain man was their lord whether they wanted him to be or not. But the disciples weren't forced to serve Jesus. They wanted him as their lord.

They believed God had made Jesus Lord of all the world. They were glad about this for they knew from experience how kind Jesus was. They knew also how powerful he was. He was the kind of person they were glad to turn over their lives to. We can be glad he is our Lord too.

Bible reading: Acts 2:29-36

What is a lord? In what ways is Jesus our Lord? How should we act toward him if we think he is our Lord?

We want you as our Lord, Jesus. Help us to turn over control of our entire lives to you. Amen.

Something to do:

Make a list of people who have some power over you. Compare the power Jesus has, and how you act toward these people and toward Jesus.

When did people last join your congregation? How many were there? What is the largest number that ever joined at one time?

3,000 BAPTISMS

In one day about 3,000 people were baptized and became Christians. They did it after hearing Peter tell about Jesus, especially that he had come to life again after being crucified. It happened on the Day of Pentecost. These people became Christians because the Holy Spirit was working in them, mysteriously like the wind, and yet with great power.

When the people heard what had happened to Jesus—how he had been killed as a criminal by some of their own people—they were afraid and sad. "What shall we do?" they asked.

Peter told them to do two things: First, repent. This means to tell God you're sorry for what you have done that is wrong. And to be sorry enough to stop doing it. They were to tell God that they were sorry

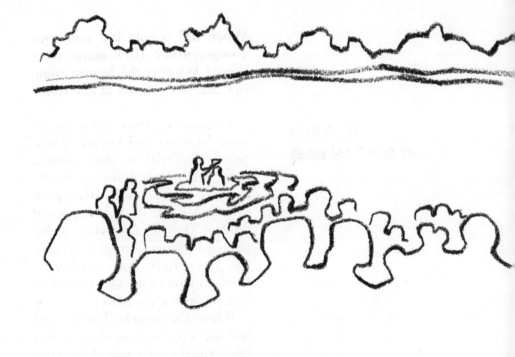

now that they hadn't listened to Jesus, and to begin believing in him as their Lord.

The second thing was for them to be baptized in the name of Jesus. This would be their way of letting the Holy Spirit come into their lives. He would forgive their sins, making them pure, and would bring them into God's kingdom.

This is still the way it happens. When people repent of what they are doing wrong, when they are baptized in the name of Jesus, the Holy Spirit comes into their hearts, forgives the wrong they have done, and makes them God's children.

Bible reading: Acts 2:37-41

Why did the people ask what they should do? What did Peter tell them? What did the Holy Spirit do for them?

We thank you that you have come into our lives, Lord. Help us always to be your people. Amen.

A verse to remember:

"Repent, and be baptized every one of you in the name of Jesus Christ for the forgiveness of your sins" (Acts 2:38).

What do you most often call your minister: pastor, reverend, parson, preacher? What do these titles mean?

PEOPLE GIFTS

God sometimes gives unusual gifts. Some of his gifts to us are people. That is, he sees to it that people who can do things that will be helpful to us are on hand when we need them. Some of these "people gifts" are in your congregation and community.

The Bible lists several. 1) Apostles. Most of these men traveled with Jesus and were trained by him. Their job was to tell everyone what they had learned about the love of Jesus. They were gifts especially to people who lived when they did. But they are gifts to us too: they are still helping us through their words in the New Testament.

2) Prophets. Prophets aren't just people in the Old Testament who did wonderful things. There are prophets now too. A prophet can

136

be anyone who tells us what God wants us to know.

3) Evangelists. These are people who tell others the good news of Jesus and his love. They want everyone to believe in Jesus. You probably know more than one evangelist: your pastor, or your Sunday school teacher, or your mother or father or brother or sister. These can be of any age.

4) Pastors. These are people who care for others. We think first of our pastor. (As you can see, one person may be more than one gift.) But many others—doctors, nurses, social workers, neighbors, friends—can help in this job of caring for people.

5) Teachers. Everybody is a teacher. But not all teach God's will. If you do, you are a gift of God to anyone who watches you and learns from you. Of course this includes your Sunday school teacher, pastor, uncles and aunts, older brother or sister, and parents.

The Bible speaks of others who are gifts to us: people who can run an office, or give money, or encourage others. God uses many different kinds of people to give his many gifts to us. Thank God for these people gifts. And thank him when he can use you too as his gift to others.

Bible reading: Ephesians 4:11-16

What unusual gifts has God given us? Which of these gifts do you have in your congregations? Which of these people gifts do you value most in your own life?

Thank you, God, for these people gifts. Help us to allow them to serve you and us. Amen.

Something to do:

Make a list of as many people gifts God has given you as you can. Pray for each one.

137

SOMETHING FOR GOD

What kind of a gift do you think God likes most?

Would you like to do something for Jesus? When we think of all he has done for us, we naturally want to do something for him. We'd like to show our thanks for his love, his care, his forgiveness.

But how can we do this? What could we give him? What could we do for him? He has the power to do anything. Even if we could think of something—how do you go about doing something for someone you can't see?

Jesus told us how in a story about the end of the world. At that time, Jesus said, when he rules as king, he invites those who are his people to come into the kingdom with him. As he does so, he thanks them for giving him something to eat when he was hungry, for being friendly to him when he was a stranger, for visiting him when he was sick or in prison, and for giving him clothes when he had none.

138

The people he thanks are surprised: "We never saw you hungry or sick or in prison," they say.

"No," Jesus says, "but when you helped those who were in need, even the least important, you were helping me." By helping people in need they were doing what Jesus himself would do if he were on earth again. They were doing something for Jesus that he wanted.

If we do things simply because we think Jesus wants us to, something is missing. It's almost as if we do it for pay. But when we are so grateful for what Jesus has done that we want to share what he has given us with others, then Jesus is most pleased. A generous attitude of wanting to help other people is the gift Jesus likes most. And it's something only we can give him.

Bible reading: Matthew 25:34-40

Why were the people in the story surprised? How can we help Jesus? Why would we want to do this?

We remember again how much you have done for us, Jesus. We have received so much from you. Help us to share with others. Amen.

Something to do:

Do you know someone in prison? What can you do for him? Or do you know someone who is sick? Decide how you can help him. If you know of no one in need, talk about how you can find out about them.

WITNESSES

What is one thing you witnessed (or saw) today?

In every courtroom trial there are witnesses. These are people who are asked to tell what they saw. What they say helps the judge or jury decide what really happened—who is right and who is wrong.

You are a witness too. Every day you are asked to tell what you know about Jesus. People listen to what you say and decide whether it is true or not—and then make up their mind whether or not to believe in Jesus.

It may be that no one asks you any questions. They may just watch how you act—how helpful you are, how you treat other people. On the basis of what they see they may decide to learn more about the Jesus you believe in or the church to which you belong.

At times someone will ask you whether you think something is right or wrong, or what your

140

church is all about, or what you think of Jesus. When you answer you are a witness for—or against—Jesus.

When the court says someone is to be a witness, he can't decide he'd rather not do it. He has to tell what he knows. We don't really have any choice either. "You will be witnesses," Jesus told his disciples. If we are Christians we don't have to decide whether or not we'll do it; it's natural. If we don't believe in Jesus we are witnesses also—against him. One way or the other, we are witnesses.

Jesus said the disciples would start witnessing right in the city where they lived—in Jerusalem. Then they would be witnesses in the state of Judea, and in the neighboring state of Samaria. And finally in the farthest corner of the world.

We too start out as witnesses right where we are. As we grow and travel we can be witnesses in other places. Those who love Jesus look forward for chances to tell others how great he is, whether it is right in their own house, or down the block, or on the other side of the world.

Bible reading: Acts 1:8

What is a witness? How can we be witnesses for Jesus? Where can we do this now?

We want to tell people about you, Jesus. Help us to do this always in the best way. Amen.

A verse to remember:

"You shall receive power when the Holy Spirit has come upon you; and you shall be my witnesses in Jerusalem and in all Judea and Samaria and to the end of the earth" (Acts 1:8).

A COMMAND

What's the best way to let people know you're a follower of Jesus?

Some people don't seem to want anyone to know they are followers of Jesus. They don't care to have anyone see them praying or reading a Bible. They try not to act too religious. They never talk about Jesus or what they think of him. Maybe they are afraid that someone might make fun of them.

The Bible says if we are God's people we should say so. That's only natural. It seems strange to be ashamed to admit we love the greatest person who ever lived.

But to say it in words isn't the only way to tell people we're disciples of Jesus. It *is* important, but just to say we believe in Jesus may not mean anything to some people. Something more than words is needed to show that we really are followers of Christ.

Jesus said, "This is how people will know you are my disciples, if you love one another." He even

commanded us: "Love one another." And he told us how much: "As I have loved you."

We have been learning in this book how much Jesus loves us. We know about the many things he has done and is doing for us because he loves us. If we are to love others as Jesus loves us it means we'll be doing things to help them, as he does.

If we love others we can't keep it a secret. It will show up in the way we act. Then people who see that we are kind and helpful may decide that being a follower of Jesus is a good thing. They may also say, "If that's what happens when a person follows Jesus, I should believe in him too."

Nothing could make Jesus, and the people who love him, happier.

Bible reading: John 13:34-35

Why would you want others to know that you are a follower of Jesus? What did Jesus command us? What are some ways in which you can let others know you are a Christian?

We want others to know how much you love them, Jesus. Help us to act in love toward all people, the way you act toward us. Amen.

A verse to remember:

"By this all men will know that you are my disciples, if you have love for one another" (John 13:35).